Creative Crafts
for kids

Cupcakes, Cookies, and Cakes

Tracy Nelson Maurer

ROURKE PUBLISHING

Vero Beach, Florida 32964

www.rourkepublishing.com

Author Acknowledgments: Thank you to Meg and Tommy, Tammy, Pat, and to the crews at Rourke and Blue Door.

Photo credits: All photos © Blue Door Publishing except: cover © AVAVA; Title Page © Kheng Guan Toh, DLW-Designs, Lorelyn Medina; Contents Page © Monkey Business Images; Page 4 © Monkey Business Images; Page 5 © Monkey Business Images; Page 6 © Sarah Bossert; Page 7 © Darren K. Fisher; Page 8 © Juriah Mosin; Page 9 © Oliver Hoffmann; Page 11 © KGJS; Page 21 © Anya Ponti; Page 30 © Ruth Black

Editor: Meg Greve

Cover and page design by Nicola Stratford, Blue Door Publishing

Library of Congress Cataloging-in-Publication Data

Maurer, Tracy, 1965-
  Cupcakes, cookies, and cakes / Tracy Maurer.
      p. cm. -- (Creative crafts for kids)
  Includes index.
  ISBN 978-1-60694-346-5 (hard cover)
  ISBN 978-1-60694-508-7 (soft cover)
  1. Cake--Juvenile literature. 2. Cupcakes--Juvenile literature. 3.
Cookies--Juvenile literature. I. Title.
  TX771.M31684 2009
  641.8'653--dc22
                                    2009010702

Printed in the USA

www.rourkepublishing.com - rourke@rourkepublishing.com
Post Office Box 643328 Vero Beach, Florida 32964

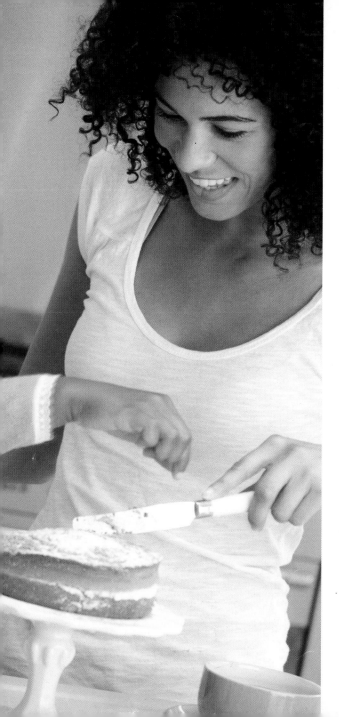

contents

How old are birthday cakes?

Ancient Greeks brought cakes to the temple of Artemis, their moon goddess. They burned candles on the cakes to shine like full moons. This could have started the birthday cake **tradition**, but no one knows for sure.

Kitchen Art

Cookies, cakes, and cupcakes are the baker's **canvas**. Decorate these sweet treats for birthday parties, holiday celebrations, or to make any day special. Use the projects in this book to help inspire your tasty designs.

Think Theme

Parties often have a theme that will help you decide how to design your treats.

Here are some popular themes:

- aliens
- animals
- beach fun
- cooking
- cowboys
- dress-up
- fish
- hit music
- monsters
- pirates
- princesses

See how much fun you can have decorating cupcakes!

Kitchen Gear

You can probably find most of these items already in your kitchen. Gather your gear before you start a recipe.

- clean scissors
- cupcake papers
- flat spatula
- measuring cups and spoons
- mixing bowls and large spoons
- **offset spatula** or butter knife
- plastic zippered storage bags
- rolling pin or clean, smooth jar
- round cake pan or muffin pan
- wax paper
- wooden toothpicks

Your Art Tools

Most decorating supplies are available at your grocery store. In addition to premade cake mixes and frostings, shop for gel icing, food coloring, coconut flakes, and colorful candies, such as string licorice, peppermints, or gumdrops!

TIP

If you cannot find the exact frosting color you want, mix food coloring with white frosting.

Remember:
blue + yellow = green
red + yellow = orange
red + white = pink
red + blue = purple

TIP

Visit a party supply store for fancy sprinkles, small plastic toy decorations, or special pastes for coloring frosting.

The Kitchen Designer's Rules:

Rule #1: Before you begin, read through the entire recipe and instructions.

Rule #2: Check that you have the correct supplies and ingredients.

Rule #3: Allow several hours to chill your baked items before decorating.

Rule #4: Always ask an adult to help with baking and cutting.

Rule #5: Clean up when you finish.

Safety Tips:

- Ask an adult before you start any of the projects in this book.
- Make sure there is an adult present when you are baking.
- Do not leave any sharp objects out where younger hands can reach them.

Try Baking at Home

You can use premade dough or cake mixes from the store for this book's projects. Or, ask an adult to help you bake at home.

Allow cookies to cool before decorating, or your frosting or gel could melt.

Grandma's Sugar Cookie Recipe

3/4 cup (172 grams) soft butter
1 cup (192 grams) white sugar
2 eggs
1/2 teaspoon (2.5 milliliters) vanilla extract
2-1/2 cups (248 grams) all-purpose flour
1 teaspoon (3.7 grams) baking powder
1/2 teaspoon (2.5 grams) salt

1. Mix butter and sugar in a large bowl until smooth. Beat in eggs and vanilla. Stir in the flour, baking powder, and salt. Cover and chill dough in the refrigerator.

2. Preheat oven to 400 degrees Fahrenheit (200 degrees Celsius). Roll out dough and cut into shapes. Place cookies about 1 inch (2.5 centimeters) apart on an ungreased cookie sheet.

3. Bake six to eight minutes until golden. Cool before decorating.

Let's get baking!

i  You Cookies

Tell your friends and family how you feel. Share these cookies on Valentine's Day or try them in other colors for someone special any day!

Here's How:

1. Ask an adult to preheat the oven to the recommended temperature.

2. Put wax paper over your flat work area. Sprinkle it with flour.

3. Put a handful of dough on the wax paper. Cover and chill the remaining dough until you need more.

4. Sprinkle flour on the rolling pin to help keep the dough from sticking. Roll out the dough until it is thinner than a pancake.

9

7. Gently move each heart to a **greased** pan using a spatula. Fill the pan, leaving 1 inch (2.5 centimeters) between hearts. Bake as directed. Cool for one hour.

5. Press the cookie cutter through the dough.

6. Make as many hearts as you can from the rolled dough.

8. Spread white frosting on each heart.

9. Use the gel icing to draw a smaller heart in the center of the cookie. Fill it with the red candies.

10. Write I above the heart and the person's name below the heart.

Add a border with lines or dots.

- knife or spatula
- small mixing bowl
- toothpick

Ingredients:

- yellow and red food coloring
- cinnamon graham crackers
- premade white frosting
- pink gel icing
- white chocolate chips
- yogurt covered raisins
- chow mein noodles

12

Critter Cookies

Invite your friends to a Mouse in the House Party, and share your favorite books or movies that have mice **characters**. These cute critter cookies add to the mice theme.

Here's How:

1. Carefully break the graham crackers into rectangles.

2. Set aside 2 tablespoons (29 grams) of white frosting. In a small bowl, mix 1 cup (230 grams) of white frosting with two drops of yellow and one drop of red food coloring. Add more yellow or red to make your frosting orange.

3. Spread orange frosting on each rectangle to look like cheese.

A little food coloring goes a long way. completely mix one drop at a time.

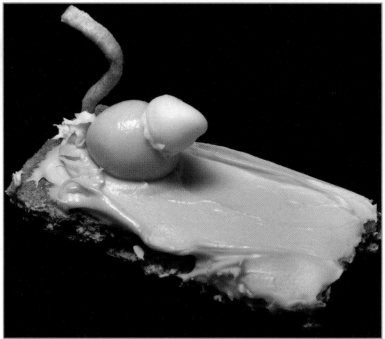

4. To make the mouse, dab white frosting on the flat end of a white chocolate chip. Attach it to the flattest end of a yogurt raisin.

5. Dab more orange frosting near a corner of the cracker and attach the mouse there.

6. Dab white frosting on the yogurt raisin end and attach a chow mein noodle upright for a tail.

7. Use a toothpick and white frosting to shape each tiny ear.

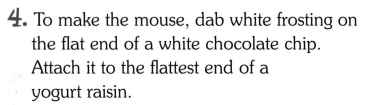

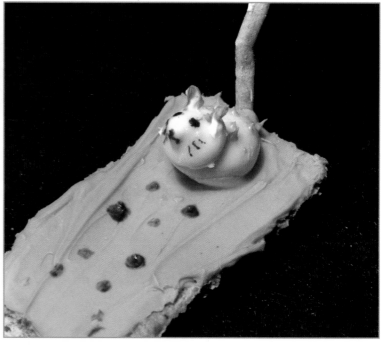

8. With the gel icing, make two tiny dots on the chip for eyes. Chill the cookies for 30 minutes before serving.

For a brown critter, use chocolate chips and chocolate-covered raisins.

Add dots, whiskers, or fangs to create the wildest mouse in the house!

- toothpick
- offset spatula
- small mixing bowl
- clean scissors

Ingredients:

- package of chocolate-covered cookies with peanut butter or marshmallow mounded centers
- premade white frosting
- red food coloring
- black string licorice, cut into 1-inch (2.5-centimeter) strips
- black gumdrops
- mini chocolate chips

Ladybug cookies

Tuck these ladybugs on a plate with silk flowers. To add to the garden theme, serve the cookies with a new trowel. Wash and dry the flowers and trowel first.

Here's How:

1. In a small bowl, mix 1 cup (230 grams) of white frosting with two drops of red food coloring.

2. Spread frosting over the rounded top of a cookie for the ladybug's back.

3. Use a toothpick to draw a line down the center of the ladybug's back.

4. Put three mini chocolate chips on each side of the line for spots.

5. The gumdrop is the ladybug's head. Use the toothpick to poke two small holes onto the top of the gumdrop. Stick one piece of licorice into a hole for each **antenna**.

6. Dab frosting on the back side of the gumdrop. Press the gumdrop to the cookie to attach it.

7. Stick three licorice legs into each side.

8. Chill for at least an hour before serving.

17

You Will Need:

- toothpicks
- knife
- fork
- clean scissors

Ingredients:

- round cake, chilled
- premade white frosting
- one black gumdrop
- two green gumdrops
- pink gel icing
- colorful candy sprinkles
- black string licorice

Kitty Face Cake

Most cake mixes and recipes make two 8-inch or 9-inch (20.5-centimeter or 23-centimeter) cakes. Wrap the second cake in plastic and freeze to decorate later.

Here's How:

1. Imagine that your cake has a clock face. Put a toothpick at 11 o'clock and one at 1 o'clock.

2. Ask an adult to cut an arc, or a curved line, from the 11 to the 1. The cutout piece should be about 5 inches (12.7 centimeters) at its widest. The cutout leaves a pointy ear on each side of the face.

3. Slice the cutout piece in half through the middle. Place the flat edges opposite of each other for a bow.

4. Spread frosting over the top and sides of the cake face and bow. Drag a fork through the frosting on the head to make lines like fur.

5. Draw triangles inside the ears with the pink gel icing.

6. Ask an adult to slice the ends off each green gumdrop. Use the gumdrop ends for the eyes by placing them on the cake where they should be.

7. Use the black gumdrop for the nose. Scatter the sprinkles on the bow.

8. Snip the licorice string to fit the long way on each green gumdrop circle. Dab frosting on the licorice to attach it to the gumdrop. Wipe off extra frosting.

9. Snip eight licorice pieces to 4 inches (10 centimeters) each for whiskers. Place three sideways near the left side of the nose and three sideways near the right side of the nose.

10. To make the mouth, curve the last two licorice pieces into a J shape. Place one J under the pink gumdrop nose. Place the other J backwards next to the first J.

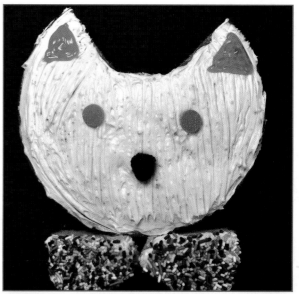

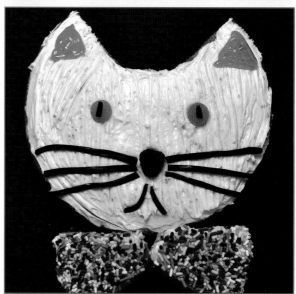

- wax paper
- clean scissors
- rolling pin
- freezer bag

Ingredients:
- baked cake in round, square, or rectangle shape; chilled
- white spray icing
- blue spray icing
- 7 graham crackers
- 3 gumdrops
- chewy fish candy

Beach Cake

Create a fun beach scene on your cake. Try different beach and sea decorations to fit your party theme.

Here's How:

1. Spray blue icing over part of the cake for the ocean. Spray in wiggly lines to create waves.

2. On the other part, pat a thin coat of crushed graham crackers to shape the beach. (Crush graham crackers inside a freezer bag using a rolling pin or other heavy object.)

3. Spray white icing along the blue ocean to make the surf line.

4. On wax paper, flatten the gumdrops with the rolling pin. Cut the flat gumdrops into stars for sea stars.

5. Lay the chewy fish candies in the ocean.

TiP

If you don't want to buy a shaped cake pan, you can bake a sheet cake and cut it into the shape you want with a large cookie cutter. Then frost and decorate.

Make Your Own Frosting

Instead of premade sugar frosting, try this frosting recipe for **homemade** decorating.

3 cups (390 grams) **powdered sugar**
1/2 cup (115 grams) softened butter
1/2 teaspoon (2.5 milliliters) vanilla extract
1 teaspoon (3 grams) **cream of tartar**
1/4 cup (60 milliliters) milk
large mixing bowl

1. Mix powdered sugar and butter until smooth.

2. Add vanilla and stir.

3. Blend in the milk one teaspoon at a time to make a creamy frosting.

You Will need:

- clean scissors
- small mixing bowl
- freezer bag
- rolling pin

Ingredients
- chocolate cupcakes, chilled
- 2 cups (180 grams) chocolate cookie crumbs
- 1 cup (180 grams) chocolate chips
- 1/2 cup (76 grams) raisins
- premade chocolate frosting
- chewy worm candy

22

Bucket of Dirt Cupcakes

Bucket of dirt cupcakes work well for garden or **construction** party themes. Ask your guests to decorate their own cupcakes. The design is easy to make, even for small hands. Serve and eat your cupcakes with tiny toy shovels or buckets.

Here's How:

1. Spread frosting on the top of each cupcake.

2. Mix cookie crumbs, chocolate chips, and raisins in a small bowl. Sprinkle this mixture on the frosting and pat into place.

3. Cut worms in half. Dab frosting on the cut end and stick into the cupcake top. Use one to four worms on a cupcake.

To make crumbs, put a few cookies in a plastic zipper freezer bag. Use a rolling pin to break the cookies into small bits. This works for graham crackers, too.

You Will need:

- clean scissors
- 1 zipper storage bag

Ingredients:
- cupcakes, chilled
- 1 cup (76 grams) coconut flakes, tinted green
- red fruit leather strips
- yellow gumdrop or chewy worm candy
- gel icing or decorating shapes
- black string licorice, cut into 1-inch (2.5-centimeter) strips
- candy flowers, often sold in birthday cake decorating kits

Butterfly Cupcakes

These pretty butterflies look especially beautiful when you make them in many different colors.

Here's How:

1. Spread frosting on each cupcake top.

2. Pat tinted coconut onto frosting.

3. Stick a candy flower into the frosting, near the edge.

4. Squish a gumdrop and rub it between your hands until it is long like a worm. Place this gumdrop body on the frosting.

5. Fold the strip of fruit leather in half the long way. Starting at the folded edge, cut a shape like a wing about 2 inches (5 centimeters) long. Open the fruit leather and cut it in half the long way. Put one piece on each side of the long gumdrop for wings.

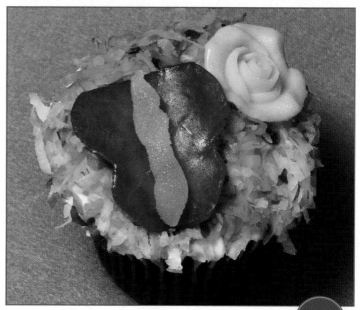

6. Stick 2 small licorice strings in front for each antenna.

7. Use gel icing or cake sprinkles to add designs to the wings.

How to Tint Coconut

1 cup (76 grams) flaked coconut
2 drops liquid food color or 1 tablespoon (7 grams) cocoa powder for brown color
1 zipper storage bag

1. Place the coconut and food coloring into the bag.

2. Shake until the coconut is evenly tinted.

Here are some ideas for using tinted coconut in your decorating:

• green coconut for grass
• pink coconut for inside ears or bows
• brown coconut for fur

Little Gingerbread House

- 4 inches (10 centimeters) duct tape
- small empty milk carton
- small mixing bowl
- zipper plastic bag
- clean scissors

Ingredients:

- 10 graham crackers
- royal icing
- assorted candies
- coconut flakes
- assorted gel icing and packaged frosting tubes

A small milk carton holds up your house while you work on it. This project takes at least a day to make. Be sure to cover your table for the construction mess!

Here's How:

1. Wash out a small milk carton. Completely dry the inside and outside of the carton. Seal the top with duct tape.

2. Put a small amount of royal icing into a plastic bag. Snip a tiny corner. Twist the upper part of the bag to press icing out of the little hole as you work. Store extra in an airtight container.

Royal icing is usually made with raw egg whites. It is very dangerous to eat uncooked eggs. Meringue powder is safe to use and yummy to eat when you finish your project!

Royal Icing

6 tablespoons (90 milliliters) water
6 teaspoons (18 grams) Wilton **meringue powder** (available at baker's supply stores or online)
5 cups (651 grams) powdered sugar

1. Blend the meringue powder and water until smooth.

2. Add half of the meringue mix to the powdered sugar.

3. Continue adding small amounts of meringue mix until your royal icing is thick like peanut butter or putty. Keep it covered. When it dries, royal icing turns into a hard glue.

3. Break two graham crackers to fit the sides of the milk carton. Put royal icing on the back of each cracker to glue it to the carton. A space at each corner is fine.

4. For the front and back, ask an adult to help cut two angles on the top of each graham cracker, making a peak that fits the milk carton. Use royal icing on the back to glue it to the carton.

5. Use a full cracker for each side of the roof. Add extra icing on the edges of the side walls where the roof pieces attach. Again, a wide space between the two crackers is okay. Let the structure set for two hours.

6. Add candies to decorate your roof, walls, doors, and windows. Let the house harden overnight.

7. Place your house on cardboard covered with aluminum foil. Use royal icing sprinkled with coconut flakes to make a snowy yard. Add a gumdrop fence or three stacked mini marshmallows for a snowman.

T i P

Any candy can add a fun touch to your kitchen artwork. Here are some favorites to try.
- hard candies, such as peppermints
- candy canes
- large twist licorice
- tiny red cinnamon candies
- gumdrops
- jelly beans
- colored chocolate or fruit candies
- miniature marshmallows
- string licorice

Set the Table

Think about how you will display and serve your finished work. Fit a cupcake into a cup for each guest to decorate. A **doily** on a colored paper plate or bright **cellophane** wrap tied with a bow might look nice. Set the table for guests and enjoy eating your art!

Try decorating these:
- bowls of pudding
- brownies
- graham crackers
- muffins
- pancakes
- pies
- store-bought cookies

Glossary

antenna (an-TEN-uh): an insect body part used to sense things

canvas (KAN-vuhss): a surface for creating a work of art

characters (KA-rik-turs): people in a story

construction (kuhn-STRUHK-shun): building

cream of tartar (KREEM uhv TAR-tuhr): a powder made from an acid for baking and cooking

greased (GREESST): made slick by rubbing or spraying butter or margarine

homemade (HOME-MADE): made from basic ingredients and not from a premade mix or dough

meringue powder (mah-RANG POW-dur): a powder for cooking and baking made from the white parts of eggs to avoid using raw eggs

offset spatula (off-SET SPACH-uh-luh): a kitchen tool with a bent blade for spreading toppings

powdered sugar (POU-durd SHUG-ur): white sugar ground to a fine powder, also called confectioner's sugar

tradition (trah-DI-shun): a custom or way of doing something that has been passed from parent to child over many years

index

Websites to Visit

http://familyfun.go.com/recipes/
http://www.foodnetwork.com/
http://www.kids-party-paradise.com/
http://www.funroom.com/

About the Author

Tracy Nelson Maurer enjoys baking and cooking for birthday parties or for any reason at all! She has written more than 60 nonfiction books for children. Tracy lives with her family near Minneapolis, Minnesota.